REX CONWAY'S
EASTERN
STEAM JOURNEY
VOLUME TWO

The
History
Press

First published 2010

The History Press
The Mill, Brimscombe Port
Stroud, Gloucestershire, GL5 2QG
www.thehistorypress.co.uk

British Library Cataloguing in Publication Data.
A catalogue record for this book is available from the British Library.

ISBN 978 0 7524 5492 4
Typesetting and origination by The History Press
Printed in Malta.

Manufacturing managed by Jellyfish Print Solutions Ltd

Contents

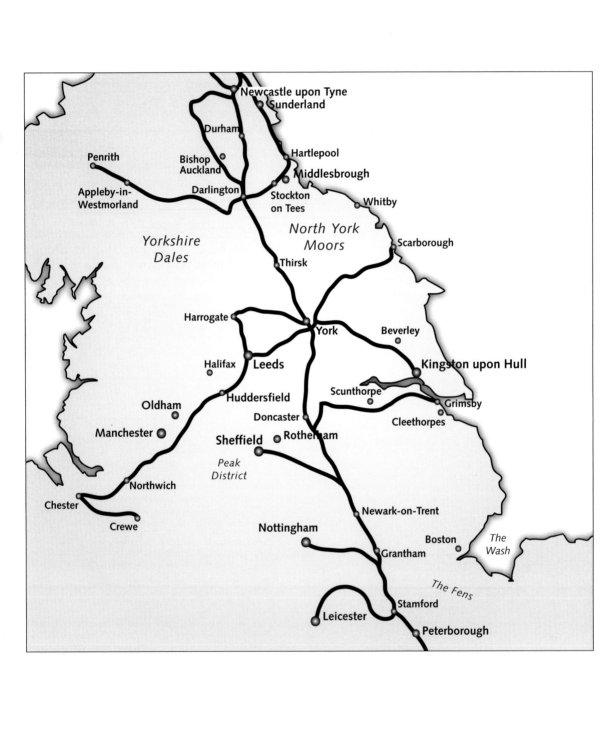

Introduction

Having completed our *Eastern Journey Volume One* from Liverpool Street to the East shores of our island – via such places as Stratford, Cambridge, Ipswich, Yarmouth and many more locations, including many branch lines – we eventually made our way to Peterborough. This book, Volume Two, takes us through a very different landscape, much more industrialised than East Anglia, which is more devoted to farming and leisure activities with its many holiday locations.

The main lines were not straight for more than a few miles, and high speeds were not possible. The East Coast Main Line beyond Grantham, which this book covers, is of course a well known race track where the World Speed Record for Steam was achieved. We visit the main Eastern Region works at Doncaster and Darlington. We will then leave the ECML to visit many dock and industrial towns on the shores of the North Sea, before eventually completing our journey in Newcastle. I have enjoyed writing and selecting the photographs for this book and I hope when you have finished reading it, you will feel you have made a worthwhile journey.

Rex Conway, 2010

A4 no. 60021 *Wild Swan* leaving Stoke tunnel, a location we shall be visiting again later.

Rex Conway's Eastern Steam Journey

O ur small band of enthusiasts are now back in Peterborough. We needed a rest after our hectic journey from Liverpool Street all around East Anglia, which was recorded in Volume One of our *Eastern Steam Journey*, so by mutual consent we gave ourselves a couple of weeks off. Our films were processed with many pleasing photographs but now it is time to start the second part of our eastern journey. Firstly, we have secured a permit to visit New England shed (Peterborough) so that is where we start. New England, with over two hundred locomotives, is one of the biggest sheds in the country. Virtually all types of locomotives can be seen, from A4s right through to small tanks. Having taken many photographs on shed and savoured the smells that surround a steam engine (which enthusiasts would bottle if they could), we must now must make our way back to Peterborough station to catch our train. The shed is about a one-mile walk from the station, so we had better get a move on.

A4 no. 60034 *Lord Faringdon* ready for duty on New England shed.

Another A4 on New England shed, no. 60012 *Commonwealth of Australia*.

Thompson 4–6–0 B1 no. 61097 weighing over 120 tons. They were well liked locos and can be seen all over the Eastern Region.

A1 4–6–2 no. 60127 *Wilson Worsdell*, a Heaton engine, probably being prepared to work an express back to Newcastle.

While on Peterborough station awaiting our train, we hear the station announcer telling passengers that the next arrival is the train to Leicester, where the Great Central Railway locos from Marylebone to Nottingham can be seen at Leicester Central. The line from Peterborough to Leicester, however, terminates at Belgrave Road – an impressive station opened in 1899 by the GCR. During the Second World War, well over two hundred special trains arrived in Leicester, carrying evacuated soldiers from Dunkirk. Special washrooms were set up on platforms so that the soldiers, who had left Dunkirk under terrible conditions, could at least have a wash to help them feel a little better.

Thompson B1 4–6–0 no. 61041 arriving at Belgrave Road.

A rather older loco at Belgrave Road, J6 0–6–0 no. 64235, at the head of a local stopping train.

Three photographs taken on the Great Central line near Whetstone, varying from a freight train, a local stopper and an express on its way north to Nottingham.

B16 4–6–0 no. 61440, designed by Raven in 1920 for the North Eastern Railway, heading a mixed freight.

A5 4–6–2T no. 69833 built in 1911 by Robinson for the GCR. It was rebuilt in 1925 with detail differences.

A3 4–6–2 no. 60065 *Knight of the Thistle* with either bad coal or a bad fireman, given the amount of black smoke coming from the chimney.

A2 4–6–2 no. 60508 *Duke of Rothesay* north of Peterborough in 1954. The first Duke of Rothesay was David Stewart, the dukedom having been created in 1398. On the death of David Stewart, his son James became King James of Scotland, and from then on the heir apparent became the Lord of the Isles, a title held by the present Prince Charles.

We are on our way now, crowding to the windows in the hope that something else has arrived on New England shed which we shall shortly be passing on our way north. Parts of the yard can be seen from the train but there's nothing new on shed since our visit a short time ago.

A2 4–6–2 no. 60511 *Airborne* pulling away from Peterborough.

With speed steadily increasing, the ex-Midland & Great Northern Railway line will bear off to the left and cross back over the line we are on before making its way back to M&GNR territory via Wisbech. We shall shortly pass through Walton where another junction on the right leads to more M&GNR territory and Spalding.

K3 2–6–0 no. 61849 near Walton with a freight train carrying a through freight headcode, possibly on its way to London.

Also near Walton is V2 2–6–2 no. 60910, this time with an express freight headcode.

After Walton we settle back on the cushions, perhaps have a sandwich and a drink, and listen to the more knowledgeable among us regarding the next stretch of line. There won't be much for us to photograph as we will be steaming at high speed, approaching the area where world records for steam haulage were made.

A1 4–6–2 no. 60118 *Archibald Sturrock* near Essendine. Archibald Sturrock, born in Dundee in 1816, rose to the exalted position of Locomotive Superintendent of the GNR. Prior to taking that position he was assistant to Daniel Gooch on the GWR from 1840 to 1850. He had a long life and died in 1909.

And here we are, the world-beating A4 no. 60022 *Mallard* near Little Bytham. It was on 3 July 1938 that the LNER, no doubt at the instigation of Sir Nigel Gresley, set out with a train of seven coaches (which included a dynamometer coach) weighing 240 tons with *Mallard* at the front weighing a further 160 tons – giving an overall weight of 400 tons. *Mallard*'s crew were driver Duddington and fireman Bray, with many experts and observers on board the dynamometer. This was going to be a serious attempt to snatch the speed record back from the LMS. Through Little Bytham comes Stoke Bank and this was where *Mallard*'s speed increased to the world record for steam traction of 126mph. This photograph of no. 60022 *Mallard* is almost at the record-breaking spot and shows a plaque on the side of the boiler, commemorating the historic moment.

WD 2–8–0 no. 90432, designed by Riddles in 1943, the class was named Austerities because of the war years when everything was in short supply, especially steel. There was no question of making them pleasing to the eye, so a basic no-frills steam locomotive was born.

A3 4–6–2 no. 60105 *Victor Wild* near Little Bytham.

A1 4–6–2 no. 60148 *Aboyeur* – named after the horse that won the Derby in 1913 – leaving Stoke tunnel in a cloud of smoke and steam.

Another view of Stoke tunnel, this time with A4 no. 60029 *Woodcock* seeing the sunshine again.

We are travelling at a good speed; estimates from my fellow enthusiasts suggest somewhere between 80–90mph, which seems very fast. Then, of course, we realise that *Mallard* was travelling 40mph faster. It is then that you realise what a fantastic achievement 126mph was.

We have now passed through Corby, and next comes Great Ponton, where speed will gradually be reduced for the stop at Grantham, where hopefully we shall take a few more photographs.

A3 no. 60110 *Robert the Devil* passing Great Ponton signal-box.

Another view of an express passing Great Ponton signal-box, this time A1 4–6–2 no. 60154 *Bon Accord*.

Great Ponton also sees many freight trains heading to and from the London area. In this view is O2 no. 63932 with a ballast train.

V2 2–6–2 no. 60870 with a headcode for a fitted freight, meaning that it is fully braked throughout, and can travel at express speeds. This view is also at Great Ponton.

Entering Grantham with a goods train is A5 4–6–2 no. 69827.

At rest in Grantham station is another A5 4–6–2T, no. 69812.

Our train has now come to a halt and, with carriage doors banging, the station announcer tells passengers where the train will shortly be going. We, however, are detraining with other passengers as we are going to visit Grantham shed. Having already studied a timetable, we know we have an hour before the next train north, which we will board. To get to the shed, which is in full view of the station, takes only a few minutes. Leaving the station you turn left and then pass into a subway with the shed entrance at the end.

A2 4–6–2 no. 60523 *Sun Castle* ready for the off at Grantham.

A4 no. 60019 *Bittern* just arriving at Grantham.

A3 no. 60049 *Galtee More*, with new, German type smoke deflectors, leaving Grantham station.

V2 2–6–2 no. 60800 *Green Arrow*, the first of nearly 200 of these very successful Gresley designed engines that did superb war work. Here, no. 60800 is seen departing Grantham with 'The Northumbrian'.

A2 4–6–2 no. 60510 *Robert the Bruce* arriving at Grantham, with 'The Queen of Scots' Pullman in 1953. Robert the Bruce was born in 1274 and died in 1329. He was the first King of Scotland and legend has it that on a lonely island in Scotland, he watched a spider trying to spin a web; it tried six times, so he said to himself that if it was successful on the seventh try, he would take on the English again. The spider achieved its goal, so he took on the English again and won at the Battle of Bannockburn in 1314.

V2 2–6–2 no. 60914 waiting to depart Grantham. At the adjacent platform is A1 no. 60123 *H.A. Ivatt*.

Taken minutes after the above photograph is A1 no. 60141 *Abbotsford* while no. 60123 is still waiting to depart Grantham.

Sitting on the platform at Grantham, one of our members starts to tell us a few things about the station, in particular about a crash that occurred in September 1906. The train involved was the 8.45 p.m. mail train from King's Cross to Edinburgh. It was due to stop at Peterborough to change engines, which it did. An Ivatt 'Atlantic' hooked onto the front of the twelve carriages and a very experienced crew took charge. Station staff at Peterborough had spoken to the crew and testified that both of the men were sober. The train left Peterborough on time and was booked to stop at Grantham at 11.00 p.m. However, that night, to the bewilderment of station staff waiting to load the mail, it roared through the station at 50mph. Meanwhile, a Leicester–Nottingham goods train was crossing the main line just north of Grantham station. The express collided with the freight and became derailed, as did nine coaches, some of which rolled down an embankment. The driver and fireman were killed as were twelve others. The cause of the accident was never discovered. Our train is now approaching, so we shall soon be on our way again.

Waiting for the 'right away' at Grantham is A3 no. 60109 *Hermit*.

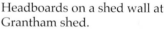

Headboards on a shed wall at Grantham shed.

We are off on our journey once more, and almost immediately there is a junction on our left that leads to Nottingham Victoria, a joint Great Northern and Great Eastern station.

O1 2–8–0 no. 63795, introduced in 1911 to a Robinson design for the GCR, works its way through Victoria station with a freight train.

Class J6 0–6–0 no. 64194, one of Gresley's early designs for the GNR, passing light engine through Victoria.

Two views of the massive Robinson 4–6–2Ts built in 1911 for the GCR, weighing in at nearly 90 tons. They were one of the heaviest tank engines to work in this country.

A5 tank 4–6–2 no. 69801 heads a local stopping train at Nottingham Victoria, 1950.

A5 tank 4–6–2 no. 69826, also at Nottingham Victoria in 1950.

J6 0–6–0 no. 64225 arriving at Nottingham Victoria with a local stopping train.

A bit further west than Nottingham is this view of C12 no. 67363 at Heanor in 1953. The crew and a porter pose for the camera.

We are once more picking up speed. After leaving Grantham we shall soon be plunged into darkness as we enter Peascliffe tunnel. On emerging we shall be approaching Barkston where there is a junction to the right leading to Sleaford, which will be well remembered by thousands of RAF recruits as the station for RAF Cranwell, one of the biggest Royal Air Force training schools in Britain.

A1 4–6–2 no. 60154 *Bon Accord* at the head of a long train passing through Barkston at speed.

Further on from Sleaford are two more views – this is of O1 Robinson 2–8–0 no. 63906 on Boston shed.

Working a coal train through Donington Road is K3 2–6–0 no. 61974.

Now seems to be a good time to check our notebooks, tidy up some of the scribbled numbers so that we can read them when we get back home, check the cameras yet again and perhaps have a bite to eat. Railway enthusiasts seem to be able to go without food and drink for hours when there is a lot happening, but when things are quiet, suddenly they are hungry and wish they had brought more sandwiches. We are now approaching Claypole.

A3 4–6–2 no. 60072 *Sunstar* near Claypole in 1951.

A3 no. 60048 *Doncaster* with small experimental smoke deflectors near the chimney, photographed between Claypole and Newark.

We are now through Newark. We did not get much chance to take any photographs as we passed straight through at good speed. There were several junctions at Newark, but we did not see any traffic on them.

Class Q6 0–8–0 was introduced in 1913, a Raven design for the NER. With driving wheels of only 4ft 7in they were powerful but not built for express speeds. This photograph is of no. 63348 near Newark.

Still travelling fast, I am informed by one of our group, who has been studying a map, that there are a couple more stations – namely Carlton-on-Trent and Crow Park – to go through before we get to Tuxford. Then we shall pass through several junctions, one to the left heading for the coalfields of Shirebrook, Bolsover and many more. A big loco shed at Langwith is home to many freight engines especially for working the coalfields. At Tuxford, a junction on the right heads east to Lincoln.

O1 Class 2–8–0 no. 63577 with a full tender and ready for duty at Langwith shed.

One of Riddles' wartime 'Austerity' locos, 2–8–0 no. 90411, also awaiting its next duty at Langwith.

A survivor from 1902 is Q1 0–8–0T no. 69929, shunting at Langwith shed.

O1 2–8–0 no. 63893 not in steam on Langwith shed.

Taking the junction in the opposite direction to Langwith will bring the traveller to Lincoln.

J67 no. 68553, an 0–6–0T designed by J. Holden for the GER in 1890, photographed on Lincoln shed in 1951. To get to the shed, which is at Brayford Wharf, you have to cross the canal via a footbridge.

A5 4–6–2T no. 69803, photographed leaving Lincoln carrying an express headcode. Perhaps it is heading for Tuxford.

We are now through Tuxford, still travelling at good speed, although before long we shall be slowing for Retford despite us not stopping. There is a major junction at Retford leading off to the left to Sheffield.

B1 4–6–0 no. 61409 was the last B1 to be listed. In the *Ian Allan abc of British Railways Locomotives*, there were over 400 of these Thompson-designed locomotives. Introduced in 1942 and weighing in at over 120 tons, they were popular with enginemen. This photograph of no. 61409 was taken at Retford.

D11 4–4–0 no. 62663 *Prince Albert* awaits departure at Retford.

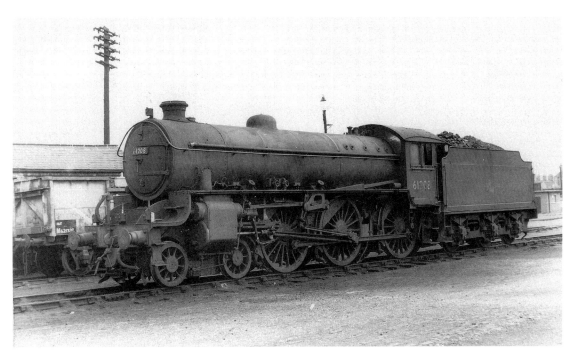

B1 4–6–0 no. 61208 on Retford shed. Retford shed, built for the GNR, is only five minutes from the station, but as we are not stopping, we shall have to hope we will see something in the yard as we pass by.

J6 0–6–0 no. 64255 carrying out an important task – to keep the railway free of unwanted growth, its heading a weed-killing train at Retford.

B1 4–6–0 no. 61151 photographed at Nunnery Junction, near Sheffield.

Sheffield Victoria was built for the GCR in 1851.

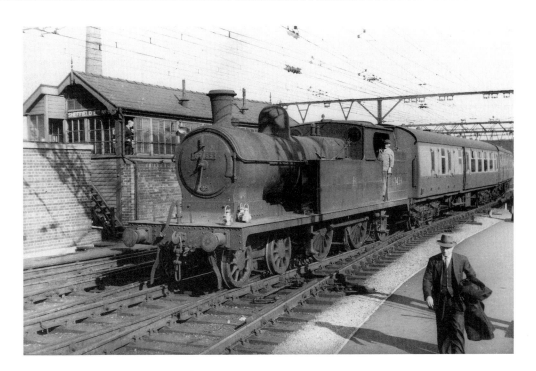

C13 4–4–2T no. 67439 arrives at Sheffield Victoria with a local passenger train.

A very elderly 0–6–2T no. 69227. It is a class N4, introduced in 1889 for the Manchester, Sheffield & Lincolnshire Railway.

On home ground, J11 no. 64329, a 41A (Sheffield Darnall) engine, works its way through Sheffield Victoria with what looks like a mixed train. It is carrying an express headcode, although I can't imagine an 0–6–0 of 1901 roaring along at high speed.

Photographed on the turntable at Darnall is O1 2–8–0 no. 63648.

About to leave Sheffield Victoria is V2 2–6–2 no. 60831.

B12 4–6–0 no. 61574 arrives at Sheffield Victoria with a two-coach train.

The Woodhead route over the Pennines was a real trial for the engine crews and their locos. From Sheffield there was not much chance of high speed, and crews knew that once they had passed Penistone it would not be long before they would have to face the dreaded Woodhead tunnel. The tunnel is three miles long. During the Second World War the route was heavily used and the tunnel was always full of smoke and steam. The crew had to cover their faces with wet handkerchiefs against the sulphurous fumes and it was always a relief to see the light at the end.

Photographed at Beeley Wood, on the Woodhead Sheffield–Manchester route, is B1 no. 61160.

C13 4–4–2T no. 67434 at the head of a three-coach local train at Beeley Wood.

This photograph is of C13 4–4–2T arriving at Penistone.

Another big shed in the Sheffield area is Mexborough 36B, almost entirely a freight loco depot with well over one hundred engines shedded there.

One of the numerous freight engines shedded at Mexborough is O1 2–8–0 no. 63723.

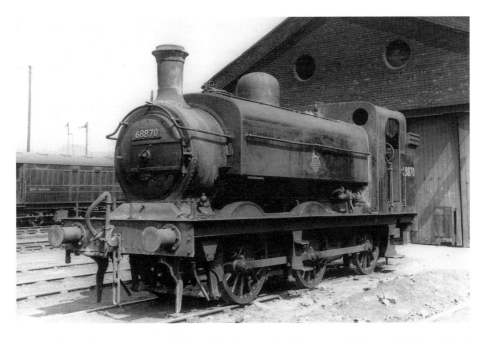

Just to show there is some variety at Mexborough, this view of J52 no. 68870 an 0–6–0 tank from 1897, built to a design by Ivatt for the GNR.

Doncaster, home of the giant Eastern Region Locomotive Works, where for decades schoolboys have stood on the platforms and seen spotless locos emerge from the works, scribbling the numbers down in notebooks. Meanwhile, older spotters would be pointing their Box Brownies, or perhaps the more advanced enthusiast would have a folding camera. No matter what the quality, as soon as they received their prints back from the chemist they would be showing all their friends the results. Doncaster works was built in 1853 for the GNR and covered an area of some 60 acres. Initially it was just for repairing locos, and it was not until 1866 that the first steam engine was built at the 'Plant', as it was known locally. Patrick Stirling was the moving force to enlarge the works to enable locos to be built. Many famous steam engines were built there, including Patrick Stirling's own 8ft Singles. The Ivatt 'Atlantics' also saw life for the first time here and later came the 'Pacifics' and of course the most famous, Gresley's world-beating *Mallard*. The last steam locomotive to leave the works at Doncaster was in October 1957.

4–6–2 A1 no. 60134 *Foxhunter*, arrives at Doncaster. A Peppercorn design, introduced in 1946, in working order it weighed 164 tons.

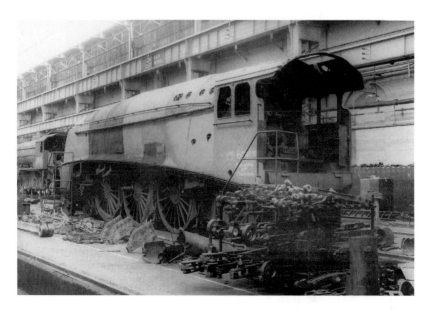

A4 no. 60010 *Dominion of Canada* under repair in Doncaster works.

Our train, having arrived at Doncaster, has come to a halt. It's time to grab our bags and cameras and rush on to the platform, armed with our passes to visit the shed and works. We shall be guided by one of our band of enthusiasts who has been here before. We are blessed with a lovely sunny day, so we will have no excuses if the photographs are not up to standard. The shed is about a 15-minute walk to the south of the station and, having presented ourselves at the offices, we are given a friendly welcome – although the expressions on our guides' faces say we must be mad to travel such long distances just to look at steam engines. We have taken what seems to be hundreds of photographs in the shed before we are then guided to the works. We see so much that it is difficult to take it all in, but it will be a pleasure to relive our experience through our photographs. In the works there are a couple of A4s with a very knowledgeable engineer working on one of them. He tells us all about the history of these superb locos and why they were built. He tells us that in 1934, Gresley talked to the board of the LNER about a German train that was streamlined, but after a visit to Germany it was decided that it would not be suitable for running on the LNER as it was only three carriages long. Wedgwood, the Chief General Manager of the LNER, and Gresley, with the board's approval, made tests using an A3 loco, and speeds of 108mph were achieved. With these tests satisfactorily completed, the A4 was born in Gresley's mind.

It was not only the locomotive that had to be built, but also seven carriages, as the LNER wanted to run a named train, 'The Silver Jubilee', to commemorate King George V's twenty-five years on the throne. The train would run between London and Newcastle.

In a matter of months, engine and carriages were ready for testing. On 27 September 1935, a special train was run from King's Cross to Barkston, just north of Grantham, conveying senior officers of the LNER and the press. It was an outstanding success with *Silver Link* setting a new speed record of 112mph

LNER A4 no. 2512 *Silver Fox* at the head of 'The Silver Jubilee' train in 1936. The name *Silver Fox* is hand-painted on the side of the boiler and underneath is a stainless-steel fox, presented by the United Steel Company.

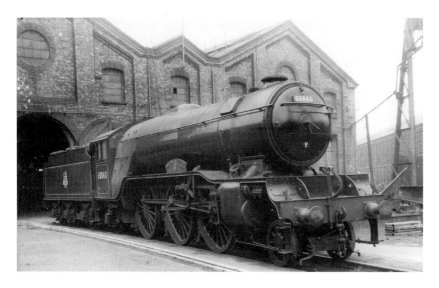

V2 2–6–2 no. 60860
Durham School
photographed at
Doncaster in 1953.

On Doncaster shed is
no. 60517 *Ocean Swell*.

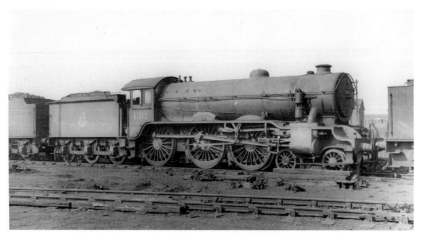

A rather tired looking
B17 no. 61612
Houghton Hall at
Doncaster. Perhaps it
is waiting to go into
the works. Houghton
Hall in Norfolk was
the stately home of
Britain's first prime
minister, Robert
Walpole. He inherited
the estate on the death
of his father in 1700.

Another three views at Doncaster, showing the diversity of locos to be seen.

A4 no. 60010 *Dominion of Canada*. Compared with the picture on page 39 (where it is seen in bits), it now looks ready to give a high speed main line run. At this stage it still had its presentation bell given on the occasion of its visit to Canada in 1937. The clapper on the bell was removed at the start of the Second World War to comply with government regulations that no bells should be rung in Britain unless it was to notify the country was about to be invaded.

J52 0–6–0ST no. 68800 on shed.

Standard class Pacific no. 70000 *Britannia* when a couple of years old. Presumably at an open day, it is obviously a big attraction.

The V2s first saw life in 1936. Designed by Gresley, they were extremely efficient. This view is of no. 60948 about to leave Doncaster station in 1949, still in its wartime grime.

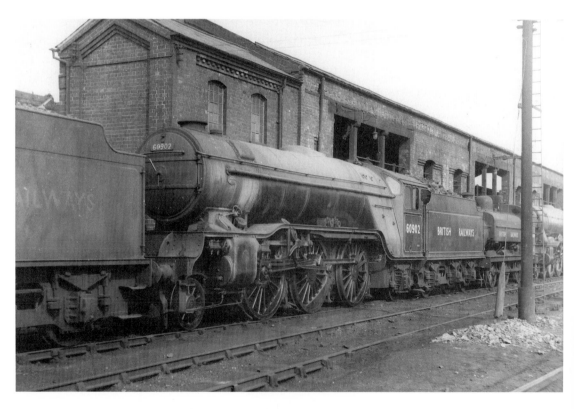

Several years later, V2 no. 60902 has its tender filled.

A2 4–6–2 no. 60525 *A.H. Peppercorn* was named after one of the last LNER designers and was fitted with the original single chimney.

A2 Pacific no. 60533 *Happy Knight* photographed on Doncaster shed showing the original style of double chimney with no rim.

We could have spent all day at Doncaster works, taking in the atmosphere, the smells and the noise. To the non-enthusiast it probably seemed like a scene from Dante's *Inferno*, but to us it was an exciting experience. Regrettably we now have to make our way back to the station as the journey must go on.

B17 4–6–0 no. 61666 *Nottingham Forest* leaves the station at Doncaster.

A3 4–6–2 no. 60048 *Doncaster* at Doncaster.

A3 no. 60066 *Merry Hampton* heads south out of Doncaster.

Back on the station, we all make a visit to the refreshment room to stock up on drinks and whatever there is on offer behind those glass display cabinets. Once satisfied, it is back out on to the platform again to wait for our train. It's not long before we hear the announcement that the next train will be for York, and another A3 rolls into sight, comes to a halt in front of us and we board rapidly. It's strange how often the front compartments are very often empty; I suppose the travelling public do not like the smells and sounds of the engine – to us it's as good as a classical symphony. Here we go, the whistle sounds and we are off!

A3 no. 60103 *Flying Scotsman* heads north out of Doncaster.

From Doncaster there is a long arm of the Eastern that reaches through Manchester all the way to Northwich and Chester. However, we won't be taking that route as we shall stay on the main line to York. I listen to those among us that know more about the area than I do. On the way to Manchester there is a little branch to Hayfield and the works at Gorton. Ordsall is also in the Manchester area.

C14 4–4–2T no. 67443 at Hayfield which is on a small branch line south-east of Manchester.

Wath freight yard is a marshalling point for vast numbers of coal wagons on the Wansborough branch, with a 2½-mile incline at 1 in 40. It needed a giant engine to push coal trains of over 1,000 tons up the bank, so Gresley and Garratt came up with the big one, 2–8–0 + 0–8–2 Beyer Garratt no. 69999 built in 1925. Weighing in at 178 tons, it was the biggest engine at work on any British railway and it is photographed here at Gorton works in Manchester. In 1848, Gorton works was built for the Manchester, Sheffield & Lincolnshire Railway. In 1858 the first locomotive was built and in 1897 it became part of the GCR. The last steam locomotive built was B1 no. 61349 and was shopped out in 1950.

Another area of Manchester that seems to have been popular with railway photographers was Ordsall. Here 4–6–2 no. 60114 *W.P. Allen* is seen in 1952.

Another photograph at the same spot is of a rather more elderly loco, J6 0–6–0 no. 64179. I would be willing to bet that the photograph was taken at almost the same time on the same day as the one above.

Again at Essendine, here is K3 no. 61872, a Hull engine, with a mixed freight train.

There are many areas near Manchester where Eastern engines can be seen. This view of B1 no. 61123 was photographed at Wakefield 25A, which of course is a Midland shed. Eastern engines were not strangers to this shed.

Back to an Eastern Region shed, Barnsley 36D, and C13 4–4–2T no. 67423 simmers quietly in hazy summer sunshine.

From Manchester, the Cheshire Lines Committee built a line through to Chester, which is about as far west as the Eastern Region extends. This view is of Northwich station. Shortly after leaving this station, the Eastern Region crosses the Midland main line to Crewe.

Another view at Northwich, this time of an 0–6–0 of 1896 vintage working a coal train through the station in 1954.

The end of the line for the Eastern Region, Chester Northgate, with N5 0–6–2T no. 69339 with a three-coach local train at the platform.

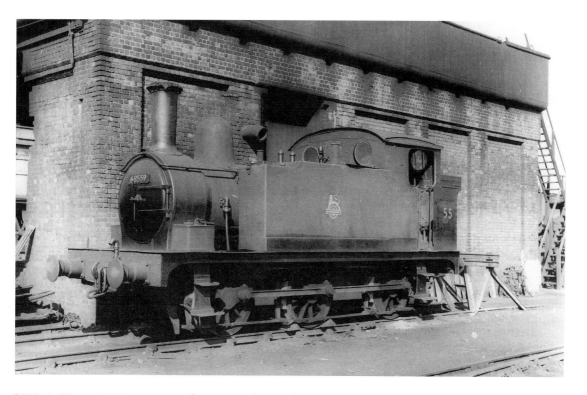

J67 0–6–0T no. 68559 resting at Chester Northgate shed 6D.

After looking at some photographs of locations where Eastern Region engines can be seen to the west of the main line, we are once again back on the line, heading for York. Our concentration now back on our route, here is K3 no. 61875 at Moat Hills to the north of Doncaster.

Also at Moat Hills is this photograph of K1 no. 62062 at the head of a mixed freight.

Looking immaculate at the head of a 'Northern Rubber Special' is record-breaker A4 no. 60022 *Mallard*, photographed north of Doncaster.

We are making good speed now that we have passed Arksey, and will soon be passing under the Hull and Barnsley line. Near this junction is A1 4–6–2 no. 60146 *Peregrine*.

The Hull and Barnsley line that we have just passed under is a very busy line, particularly for freight. Frodingham shed 36C has quite a large compliment of freight engines and is located some 25 miles from the ECML. Scunthorpe, with its huge industry, is right next to Frodingham, hence the need for so many heavy freight locos.

O2 2–8–0 no. 63945 at Frodingham in 1959.

Q1 0–8–0T no. 69927 was built by Robinson in 1902 and is a very suitable engine for working in such a heavily industrial area.

Once the above loco has done its work, shunting the heavily laden trucks into a train, it is then the turn of the B1s and the like to take the trains onto the main line to destinations in many parts of the country. A work-stained B1 no. 61328 is seen here on Frodingham shed.

On the main line near Scunthorpe is B1 no. 61215 *William Henton Carver*. In the early days of my trainspotting, and then taking photographs, I was always intrigued by names, but the chances of finding information was slim. However, I did try, and with some success I found out that Mr Carver was MP for Howdenshire in Yorkshire.

N7 0–6–2T no. 69678 photographed at Scunthorpe in 1953.

We are still on the ECML, taking refreshment while our friend with the map tells us a bit more about locations further on from Scunthorpe. The line goes through a number of junctions including one at Brocklesby. Built in 1848 for the Manchester, Sheffield & Lincolnshire Railway, Brocklesby was the nearest station to the country seat of the Earl of Yarborough, who was the chairman of the MS&LR. With his influence, the station was built in the character of his home and is thus very grand. Prince Albert was known to use the station when he opened Grimsby's first dock in 1849. A line leads off to the left to New Holland Pier on the banks of the Humber, opened in 1849, and no doubt serving some of the shipping on the river. It got its name New Holland because the Pilgrim Fathers left here for Holland. It was also home to smugglers of Holland Gin.

K3 2–6–0 no. 61941 near Brocklesby with a fitted freight, possibly on its way to or from Immingham.

Another K3, no. 61956, is seen with a passenger train at New Holland Pier with the pier in the background.

Past Brocklesby and the junction to New Holland Pier, it's only a short distance to the port of Immingham on the Humber. Immingham has a rich naval history; during the First World War it was a submarine base and the Second World War saw Lord Mounbatten with his famous ship HMS *Kelly* based there. The present dock was opened in 1913 by King George V.

K3 2–6–0 no. 61849 on its way to Immingham with a freight train, which will no doubt be exported to the Continent.

When you see this sign, you have arrived at Immingham dock.

A dock shunter, J63 no. 68206, on Immingham shed. Built in 1906 to a Robinson design for the GCR, it only weighed 37 tons, but with a short wheelbase, and wheels of only 3ft 6in, it was an ideal size for working the dock areas.

Another design by Robinson, O1 2–8–0 no. 63878, certainly not suitable for working the docks area, but ideal for heavy freight to many parts of the country.

A rather grimy and tired looking J11 0–6–0 no. 64325 waiting its turn to take another freight train from Immingham to a freight yard somewhere on the Eastern system.

A warning notice at Immingham.

O1 2–8–0 no. 63759 with fellow O1 no. 63860 on Imminghm shed.

A few miles south of Immingham is Grimsby, one of the biggest fishing ports in the British Isles. Here, 4–6–0 no. 61168 awaits the green flag before departure from Grimsby Town.

Car no. 12 of the Grimsby Electric System, which opened in the early part of the 1900s to operate between Grimsby and Immingham.

On the opposite bank of the River Humber from New Holland is Hull, a very important port. However, to get there by rail we would have to change trains at Selby, but this is not in our plans as we must press on with our journey north. Studying the map once more, and listening to one of our group who has travelled from Selby to Hull, he tells us all about the line. Just before Selby on the ECML, a line leads off to the right. This is the north-eastern line to Hull and it passes through Goole before crossing the River Ouse, which changes its name to the River Humber a few miles on. The track follows the river for quite some distance before passing through Hessle and entering the major rail centre of Hull.

K3 2–6–0 no. 61813 at the head of an express at Hessle.

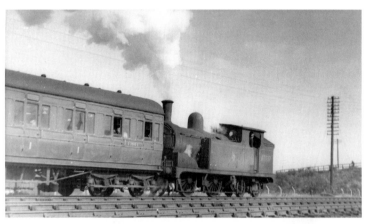

This view is of a local passenger train near Hessle with 0–4–4T G5 no. 67337 in charge. Built in 1894 to a Worsdell design, it was also later fitted with push and pull equipment.

This photograph, taken at the same spot, is of B16 4–6–0 no. 61476.

There are three loco sheds in Hull: Dairycoates (53A), Botanic Gardens (53B) and Springhead (Alexandra Dock – 53C). Dairycoates is between Hessle and Hull in a maze of lines, Botanic Gardens shed is about six minutes from Botanic Gardens station and Springhead is in the Alexandra Dock area.

Thompson designed L1 2–6–4 no. 67765, photographed in the suburbs of Hull, with a local stopping train.

J25 0–6–0 no. 65693 of 1898 vintage on shed at Dairycoates.

Also on shed at Dairycoates is N10 0–6–2T no. 69096, another veteran from before the First World War; it was built in 1902 to a Worsdell design for the NER.

Hull Botanic Gardens is the setting for this photograph of D49 4–4–0 no. 62703 *Hertfordshire*. This class of engine was designed by Gresley and the first batch were known as the 'Shires'. The second lot were named after hunts and, somewhat unsurprisingly, they were called the 'Hunt' class. Each of the 'Hunt' class had a brass model of a fox over the nameplate.

Botanic Gardens shed 53B is the location for D20 4–4–0 no. 62381. The D20s were a Worsdell design for the NER and were built in 1899.

J72 0–6–0T no. 69017, another loco that has had a long life. Built in 1897 it is seen here still at work nearly sixty years later, although here it's taking a well-deserved rest at Botanic Gardens shed.

In comparison with the above photograph of a J72, this photograph of A5 4–6–2 no. 69802, shows how massive this design by Robinson was. Weighing in at almost twice the weight of the J72, these huge tanks were equally at home with heavy freight or passenger services.

With driving wheels of only 4ft 7in, this design of A7 4–6–2T no. 69772 was not built for speed, but power. Designed by Raven for the NER it was mainly used for working freight trains from the docks and industrial areas of the Humber. It is photographed on Hull Springhead shed.

D20 4–4–0 no. 62360 dates from 1899. This view shows clearly how the NER cared for their crew's comfort with a large cab with windows. Waiting on Springhead in clean condition in 1951, this D20 is nearing the end of a long working life.

Hull Paragon, we are told by one of our enthusiast friends, is a very grand station. He continues to give us some details from a book he has in his bag which has proved a valuable source of information on our journey. The original station was rather plain and opened in 1848 for the York & North Midland Railway, but it was decided that the original station did not do much for the image of the NER which took over the Y&NMR. So, in 1905, a new train shed and booking hall were opened. The booking hall is a credit to the architect, William Bell. It is 80ft long and 70ft wide and is lit from above with large window lights while the walls are tiled in brown and cream. There is a large booking office in carved oak in this area, with twelve windows for passengers to book tickets to many distant and local stations. There are nine platforms for main line trains and five short ones for local traffic.

B1 4–6–0 no. 61038 *Blacktail* heads a fitted freight through Hull Paragon.

A7 4–6–2T no. 69791 heads a local train at Hull Paragon in 1950.

A few miles north from Hull on the North Eastern line is Cottingham, a country station where a wide variety of locos can be seen. This photograph is of one of Gresley's powerful 4–4–0 D49s, no. 62723 *Nottinghamshire*, on a passenger train at Cottingham in 1953.

We are nearly in to Selby now – the loco is slowing as we have to negotiate the station and a bascule bridge. The original station was built in 1834 for the Leeds & Selby Railway but was rebuilt in 1891 by the NER. The bascule bridge was opened in 1840 so completing the line through to York. The present bridge was opened in 1891 – its main span is 130ft and swings to allow traffic on the River Ouse to pass safely.

London to Edinburgh A4 4–6–2 no. 60009 *Union of South Africa* negotiates Selby station with 'The Elizabethan' express. Originally this train was called 'The Capitals Ltd', then in 1953, the year Queen Elizabeth II was crowned, in honour of the event, the name was changed to 'The Elizabethan'.

Crossing the famous swinging bascule bridge over the River Ouse at Selby is A4 no. 60029 *Woodcock*. It is heading the 'Tees-Tyne Pullman' between King's Cross and Newcastle.

Another A4 4–6–2, no. 60032 *Gannet*, crossing the Selby bascule bridge.

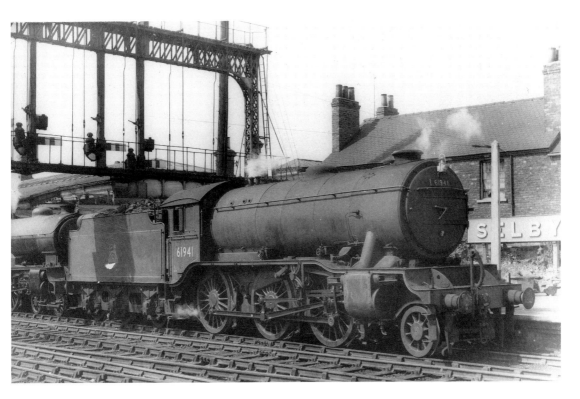

Awaiting the right away at Selby is K3 2–6–0 no. 61941. It is piloting an unidentified D49 4–4–0.

Another departure awaiting the signal at Selby is D49 *Derbyshire*.

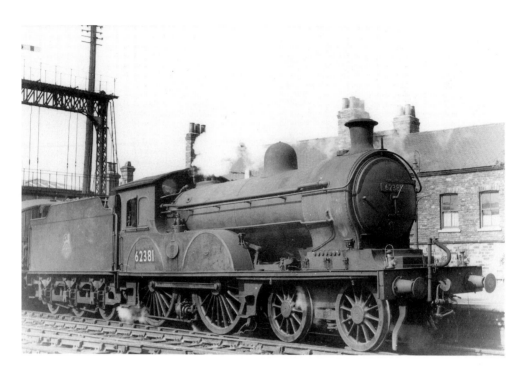

Selby is a trainspotter's heaven with many lines converging, including, of course, the East Coast Main Line. It is also a superb setting to take photographs. Here is an elderly D20 4–4–0 no. 62381 gently simmering in the summer sunshine.

At the same spot is B16 4–6–0 no. 61422 with express headlamps and a special number on the buffer beam. It is probably a holiday special.

The massive T1 4–8–0T no. 69912 was built in 1909 to a Worsdell design for the NER. They weighed getting on for 90 tons and, with their small driving wheels, they were very powerful. I am a little confused as to what it is doing at Selby. The gentleman on the ground appears to be in fireman's overalls and cap, but has a shunting pole in his hand. My question: is the engine shunting or waiting to go main-line?

Coming to a halt in Selby station in 1953 is V2 no. 60830. Looking very clean, perhaps it has recently received an overhaul.

While making a short stop at Selby I ask our friend with the map to give us some idea of where all the lines that converge on Selby come and go to. We already know about the lines heading east to Hull and Immingham and he quickly tells us that the main line to Leeds goes west from Selby. From this line there are various junctions, with one off to the left to Castleford and, at this same junction, the line heads north through Church Fenton, Ulleskelf, and onto York. Continuing straight on, you arrive in Leeds, but a short distance before Leeds at Cross Gates there is another junction that will take you to Harrogate and Knaresborough, and then back to York. Just south of Harrogate is Crimple viaduct which is over 1,800ft long and has 31 arches. It varies between 50ft and 120ft high and opened to traffic in 1848.

Working light engine through Leeds City is J39 no. 64934.

A2 4–6–2 no. 60515 *Sun Stream* having just arrived in Leeds City in 1952.

A1 Pacific no. 60133 *Pommern* on Leeds 50B Neville Hills shed, carrying the headboard 'The Harrogate Sunday Pullman'. This train ran from King's Cross to Leeds to Harrogate and finished its journey in Newcastle. It was first introduced in 1923 when the Great Eastern Railway joined the LNER at the grouping. The Pullmans had been tried on various routes with some success, so the LNER board decided to try a Pullman train that took in the spa town of Harrogate, which was very popular with the public. As the train was a success, it was decided to rename it 'The Harrogate Pullman' rather than 'The Newcastle Pullman'.

Several years later 'The Harrogate Pullman' was extended to Edinburgh, and in 1928 it was renamed 'The Queen of Scots'. Its route was also extended to Glasgow making it a 450-mile journey. This photograph is of A1 4–6–2 no. 60141 *Abbotsford* rounding the curves at Leeds Holbeck with 'The Queen of Scots'.

K3 2–6–0 no. 61808 with a loaded tender and the safety valve gently blowing. It will soon be moving off Leeds Neville Hill shed.

Neville Hill West signal-box, showing clearly memorial to those railwaymen who lost their lives in the First World War.

Just north of Harrogate is a branch line to Pateley Bridge although it's looking rather desolate and deserted in this early 1950s view.

Hill, a steam railcar built in 1905 for the GWR by Kerr Stuart on the Nidd Valley Railway. However, it was soon taken over by the Nidd Valley for operation on their Pateley Bridge to Lofthouse in Niddervale route. It was named after Sir James Hill, Lord Mayor of Bradford in 1908. The railcar was eventually sold for scrap in 1937. This photograph was taken in Pateley Bridge on 24 September 1923.

Our friend with the map, after much study, tells us of one more junction at Church Fenton where the Leeds–York line joins with the line from Knottingley to York. Ulleskelf, just after Church Fenton, is the setting for this photograph of D49 no. 62722 *Huntingdonshire*.

B16 4–6–0 no. 61437 heads a freight train near Selby.

Having just left Selby, almost immediately there is a junction to the left which will take us to our next big rail centre: York. Here we shall make a visit to York locomotive sheds, but before that we shall take advantage of this stretch of line to Chaloners Whin, just outside York. Refreshing our thirst and stoking up on refreshments – not forgetting to make sure our cameras are ready for the many locos we shall see – the carriage is buzzing with talk.

B16 no. 61445 with a freight train. It has just come off the Selby–York line at Chaloners Whin in 1956.

At the same spot and, most likely, time as the above photograph, here is B16 no. 61443 arriving at Chaloners Whin, although this time from Church Fenton.

We are now approaching York. Once again there is much activity in our compartment in readiness for leaving our train and making for the sheds as the sound of the announcer's voice, telling of our train's arrival, bounces back from the huge station roof. York station is unmistakable by the end screens which are crescent shaped with masses of glass windows. Before we come to a halt, we are told by the knowledgeable one among us that on 29 April 1942, York station and its sheds received direct hits from German bombs. Causing a partial collapse, the bombs, also including incendiaries, set fire to the roof resulting in even more damage. The King's Cross–Edinburgh express headed by A4 *Sir Ralph Wedgwood* was standing at the platform under the collapsing roof and was completely destroyed. However, the bravery and actions of many railwaymen saved most of the train's twenty carriages. We have listened to our friend, but now the brakes are on. We are at the platform and the doors open.

A1 4–6–2 no. 60153 *Flamboyant* at York.

Under the huge train shed and showing the unique end screens, here is V2 2–6–0 no. 60910.

D49 4–4–0 no. 62744 *The Holderness* is ready to leave York station in 1950. The roof canopy in the background above the tender looks very rough. Could this still be unrepaired bomb damage from years before?

Also in York station in 1950, here is B1 4–6–0 no. 61016 *Inyala*.

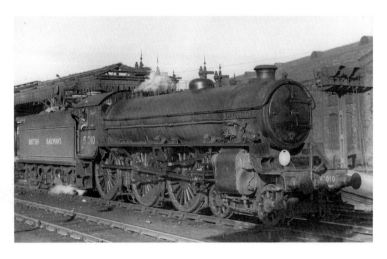

Another B1 4–6–0, no. 61010 *Wildebeeste*, at the same spot as the top picture on the same day in 1950, showing more of the roof in the background. It is well known that the railways at the end of the Second World War were short of money, and that only essential repairs were undertaken. In 1948 when British Railways came into being, the government were no better off, so it is possible that it really is leftover bomb damage.

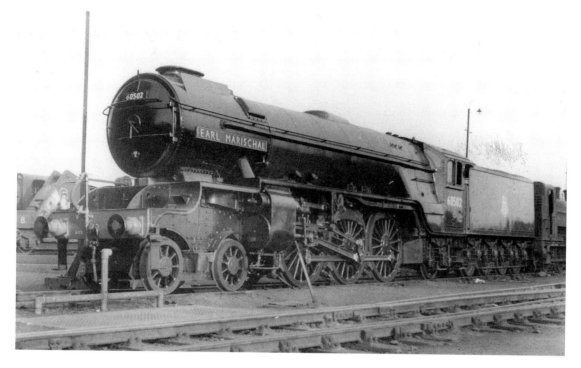

Posed in the yard is A2/2 4–6–2 no. 60502 *Earl Marischal*. This is a rebuild of a 1934 Gresley-designed P2 2–8–2.

D20 4–4–0 no. 62395, also in the yard at York shed. Express trains from the West Country via Bristol to Newcastle – usually with a Bristol 'Jubilee' working – changed engines at York. In the background can be seen Bristol 'Jubilee' no. 45651 *Shovell*.

A2 4–6–2 no. 60532 *Blue Peter* waiting to change engines at York.

J72 no. 68736 station pilot at York painted green and looking very smart.

Showing interest in the photographer, the crew of D49 no. 62734 *Cumberland* wait to depart York.

A1 4–6–2 no. 60119 *Patrick Stirling* named after the great designer of the Stirling 8ft Singles that worked the principal expresses out of King's Cross to the north. At the platform is Midland Region 'Patriot' no. 45517, an unnamed loco. Perhaps no. 60119 is waiting to take this train on to its destination.

D20 no. 62381 and an unidentified D49 leave York.

A1 4–6–2 no. 60126 *Sir Vincent Raven* leaving York. Sir Vincent Raven was the NER's Chief Mechanical Engineer between 1910 and 1924.

Heading north from York there are a number of junctions. The first, off to the left, is the line to Harrogate and Starbeck.

J39 0–6–0 no. 64942, another successful Gresley design, on Starbeck Shed.

D20 4–4–0 no. 62343, an 1899 design by Worsdell, with its tender piled high with coal. It was still earning its keep in 1955.

D49 'Hunt' class 4–4–0 no. 62727 *The Quorn*, a bit grimy, but still ready for duty on Starbeck shed.

Another D49 'Hunt' class 4–4–0 no. 62775 *The Tynedale*, near Harrogate in 1956.

From York, a line heads north towards the holiday resort of Scarborough. Many specials were to be seen on this line with thousands of holidaymakers, especially in August when most of the factories in the Lancashire and Yorkshire areas closed down for two weeks' holiday. After leaving York, the line headed north-east passing such stations as Kirkham Abbey, Castle Howard and Malton.

One of the many summer specials near Malton, headed by B1 4–6–0 no. 61158.

Another special approaching Malton is B16 4–6–0 no. 61456.

D49 4–4–0 no. 62702 *Oxfordshire* also near Malton. All three of these views were taken during the same summer months.

Three more views of Malton on the same summer Saturday in 1955.

Malton station, opened in July 1845 for the York & North Midland Railway, sees a lot of traffic in the summer months.

D49 'Hunt' class no. 62745 *The Hurworth* leaving Malton, again in 1955.

One of the large A8 tank locos, no. 69861. Originally a 4–4–4T designed by Raven in 1931, Gresley rebuilt this class as a 4–6–2T weighing in at nearly 90 tons. They also had 5ft 9in driving wheels which meant they were fairly fast and powerful – certainly capable of handling the summer passenger trains. This photograph is of another special at Malton.

Leaving Malton behind, we soon come to a junction on the left to Pickering. We carry straight on through Knapton, Heslerton, Weaverthorpe and then we come to a junction where the Filey line leaves the Scarborough line.

B16 no. 61463 with 'The Scarborough Flyer' photographed near Scarborough in 1950.

Another B16 4–6–0, no. 61421, leaving Scarborough also in 1950.

B1 no. 61049 at Scarborough in 1955.

Here are two locos on shed at Scarborough 50B on a sunny summer's day. Our eastern friend says it's always sunny in Scarborough, which is greeted with derision by the rest of our band.

B1 4–6–0 no. 61038 *Blacktail*, a York 50A engine no doubt waiting to take a train back to York.

Carrying a Scarborough 50E shed plate D49 no. 62770 *The Puckeridge*, one of the 'Hunt' class, on the turntable at its home shed.

With the gasworks signal-box in the background, K3 no. 61819 is on the move at Scarborough Shed.

Another locomotive on the move is V2 2–6–0 no. 60967 at Scarborough with a holiday special.

Another Scarborough D49 'Hunt' class on the move is no. 62751 *The Albrighton*, arriving at Scarborough with another load of holidaymakers.

D49 no. 62720 *Cambridgeshire* with another train of holidaymakers at Scarborough.

Having left Scarborough behind and heading north, the line runs very close to the coast and Robin Hood's Bay. Once past the bay, it is only a short distance to Whitby. Whitby station was built in 1847; prior to this date there was a horse-drawn railway called the Whitby & Pickering. When the Y&NMR took over this horse-drawn railway, they immediately changed it to a steam operation. George Hudson, who was chairman of the Y&NMR, wanted to develop the fishing resort of Whitby, so the station received many embellishments. The original station was renamed Whitby Town station when Whitby Westcliff station opened.

Arriving at Whitby is B1 4–6–0 no. 61020 *Gemsbok*.

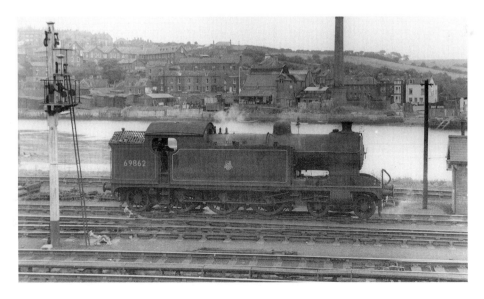

With the estuary as a background, A8 4–6–2T no. 69862 is photographed on Whitby's small shed, 50G.

Another D49 4–4–0, no. 62730 *Berkshire*, on Whitby shed.

B1 no. 61020 *Gemsbok* with a special near Whitby.

If you wanted to see the big 4–6–2T, built in the early 1900s, then Whitby was the place to visit. Here, A5 no. 69834 receives a little oiling from the fireman.

A general view of the shed yard and turntable at Whitby. A8 4–6–2T is the locomotive ready to move off shed, while no. 69834 is moving on to the turntable.

Near Thirsk is the view of K3 no. 61959, heading a local passenger train.

We are now back on the main line from York to Darlington. Apart from junctions, it's a fairly straight line, or so we are told by our map reader. The first station we shall roar through is Beningborough, followed by Tollerton and then Pilmoor where there is a junction on the left coming in from Knaresborough.

A pre-1948 view of K3 no. 1130 north of York with a mixed freight train.

Also pre-1948 is this view of B1 no. 1029 *Chamois* with a fast freight train, again north of York.

D20 4–4–0 no. 62360 at Northallerton station in 1955. There is nothing to tell it is an enthusiasts' special, but with a gentleman in casual dress on the right-hand track and others grouped around the engine, the picture has the air of a special.

B1 4–6–0 no. 61039 *Steinbok* running through Northallerton in 1956.

Our express, with our A3 sounding in superb condition, is quickly getting us to our next major location: Darlington shed and works.

A3 4–6–2 no. 60048 *Doncaster* near Darlington, with German-style smoke deflectors, which I personally thought spoiled the appearance of the A3s.

A locomotive with a long life, J21 0-6-0 no. 65103 was built in 1886 and photographed here at Darlington Bank Top in 1951. Many of this class were originally built as two-cylinder compounds, but later converted to simple locos.

We are almost into Darlington Bank Top station now, so once more we will have a quick briefing from our knowledgeable friend who knows all about stations. Bank Top station was built in 1887 by the NER to a similar design of the railway's other main stations. It has semi-circular arched roofs. A lot of red bricks were used in the construction, as were many cast iron columns, giving the station a light and airy feel. To finish the station off – and making it a Darlington landmark – a tall clock tower was added.

A8 4–6–2T no. 69866 makes a vey smoky departure from Bank Top station. The large clock can be clearly seen in the background.

Obviously with a heavy train that needs two locos, L1 no. 67777 and A5 no. 69832 leaves Bank Top station in 1951.

The other (and original) station in Darlington is North Road, built in 1842 by the Stockton & Darlington Railway – the world's first public railway to use steam traction. Passengers boarded and alighted from designated points on the line, a bit like bus stops, until proper stations were built. The Stockton–Darlington line opened in 1825, but only freight was steam-hauled – passengers had to make do with horse power. North Road station has changed very little since its opening in 1842. It has a Georgian frontage, with a tree-lined approach road.

Darlington North Road, looking a little deserted in 1954.

A different sight this time at North Road station as an enthusiasts' special has arrived, and many photographs are being taken of the engine and station. A8 no. 69855 is at the centre of attention.

We have left our train and are heading hot-foot for the works and sheds. Armed with essential passes, we hope to take many photographs and soak up the atmosphere of the works, as we did in Doncaster. The original Stockton & Darlington works was at Shildon but, as the railway grew, the site became too small, and in 1854 The S&DR locomotive superintendent and engineer wanted the works moved to a bigger location. After looking at a number of sites, it was decided to build new workshops at Darlington in the name of Shildon Works Company. Opened for business in 1863, Darlington works grew rapidly. Later, they were taken into the NER, covering an area of nearly 30 acres, and employed well over 100 men. At its busiest period, the early 1950s, the works employed nearly 4,000 men. The first loco produced was no. 175 *Contractor* in October 1864.

The erecting shop at Darlington works with D49 no. 62708 *Argyllshire* in the foreground.

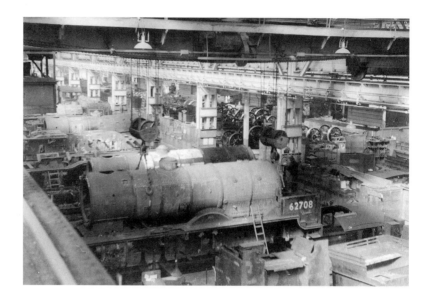

Shunting in the yard at Darlington is J21 no. 65064 of 1886 vintage, built only twenty-three years after the works opened.

Crane tank no. 68668, a works shunter at Darlington.

Push and pull fitted G5 no. 67305 looking as if it is in the middle of a paint job, as the front end is still sporting only the undercoat.

An immaculate D49 no. 62749 *The Cottesmore*, obviously after an overhaul and painting at Darlington works.

Another works job ready for the road is B16 no. 61449. It's looking equally as immaculate as the D49 above.

I have already used the words immaculate, but how else can I describe T1 4–8–0T no. 69917 as posed with no. 62749?

L1 no. 67754 at Darlington with a short local stopping train.

Our visit to Darlington works and shed has been completed, and everyone is still soaking up the atmosphere as we head back to the station to continue our journey northwards. However, before our train arrives, a discussion starts about the various lines that depart from Darlington. From North Road, a line branches off to the left to Barnard Castle and Kirkby Stephen, where the line bears to the right to Penrith, and a junction leaves for Tebay and passes under the Carlisle–Settle route.

A2 4–62 no. 60533 *Happy Knight* awaits the guard's whistle to continue its journey from Darlington.

A4 no. 60026 *Miles Beevor* is named after the LNER's chief legal advisor. He was also the chief general manager in 1947 and saw the LNER become the Eastern Region of British Railways.

Barnard Castle opened to traffic in 1861, but is looking a bit run-down in this photograph taken in 1960.

Double-heading a freight train through Barnard Castle in April 1957 is British Rail 4MT no. 76023 and 2MT 2–6–0 no. 78016.

Just after Barnard Castle is the branch to Middleton-in-Teesdale. It looks a sleepy branch line, very rural, but not much activity for a trainspotter.

A bit more activity in this view of Middleton-in-Teesdale as G5 0–4–4T no. 67258 runs around its one-coach train for the return to Barnard Castle.

Further on from the Middleton branch is Kirkby Stephen, where this 1920s view of NER 2–4–0 no. 1471 was taken.

Just after Kirkby Stephen is a small station, Smardale. This is where the Settle–Carlisle main line crosses the North Eastern line to Tebay. This photograph is of D20 no. 62360 at Hawes Junction in 1955.

Arriving at Penrith from Kirkby Stephen is J21 0–6–0 no. 65047 carrying a 51H Kirkby Stephen shedplate. It is a well known performer on this route.

Here's another J21, no. 65100, photographed on the turntable at Penrith in 1953.

Kirkby Stephen West station on a summer's day in 1955.

A 'Northern Dales Railtour' in 1955, photographed at Tebay, headed by J21 no. 65061, this time carrying a 51A Darlington shedplate. It probably hauled the railtour special from Darlington.

Another junction from Darlington is to the industrial areas of Middlesbrough through Eaglescliffe, Thornaby, Newport and Middlesbrough itself, and leads on to the coastal areas of Redcar and Saltburn.

BR 3MT no. 77012 at Eaglescliffe.

Eaglescliffe station, a junction station between Darlington and Middlesbrough, and Middlesbrough and Northallerton. A very impressive long footbridge connects the platforms. It is a very busy station, especially for freight.

A1 no. 60129 *Guy Mannering* heads non-stop through Eaglescliffe while B1 no. 61306 waits for the signal to leave with a local stopping train.

Through Eaglescliffe the line approaches Thornaby, but just before Thornaby is a junction to Stockton and the world's first passenger railway, the Stockton & Darlington. In the early days, there were not the stations or booking offices that we have today – tickets were normally sold at the local pub and you waited until a train turned up.

Q6 0–8–0 no. 63393 on Thornaby shed in 1962. These heavy locos were ideal for the heavy industry in the Middlesbrough area.

Another heavyweight, Q6 0–8–0 no. 63401, on Thornaby turntable.

B1 no. 61241 *Viscount Ridley* on the shed turntable at Thornaby – rather grimy but, nevertheless, a photograph full of atmosphere.

B16 4–6–0 no. 61441 at the head of one of the many freight trains that can be seen in the Thornaby area. Designed by Raven, the B16s appeared in 1920 for the NER. In 1937, Gresley rebuilt a few of the class with Walschaerts valve gear. In 1944, Thompson experimented with the valve gear again, but the majority of the class have run with the original Stephenson gear.

B16 no. 61458 with another freight train in the Thornaby area.

A Stockton B1 no. 61022 *Sassaby* on its way to Stillington with a freight from the Middlesbrough industrial area.

Stockton shed with J26 0–6–0 no. 65764 in the foreground. One would have to have a vivid imagination to visualise the locos that would have been on this site at the start of the railways.

Through Thornaby, the train will gradually slow for Middlesbrough. However, just before the stop comes Newport 51B. It is another shed that supplies heavy freight engines for working this heavily industrialised area. This photograph is of T1 4–8–0T no. 69910 at rest on Newport shed.

A2 no. 60520 *Owen Tudor* on the main line at Newport. In the background is Newport shed.

Middlesbrough station was built in a Gothic style with pointed arches. Regrettably, the Second World War saw it suffer a great deal of bomb damage, and it lost a lot of its character with concrete replacements for the damage.

Middlesbrough shed is home to V1 2–6–2T no. 67685.

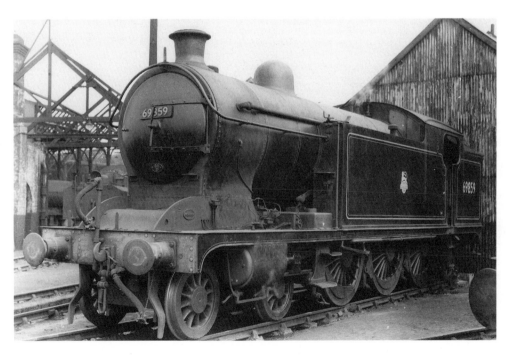

A8 4–6–2T no. 69859 simmers quietly on Middlesbrough shed in 1955.

Another of the big A8 4–6–2Ts, a Gresley rebuild of Raven's 4–4–4T, introduced in 1913. Middlesbrough shed is looking in a run-down state in this 1953 view.

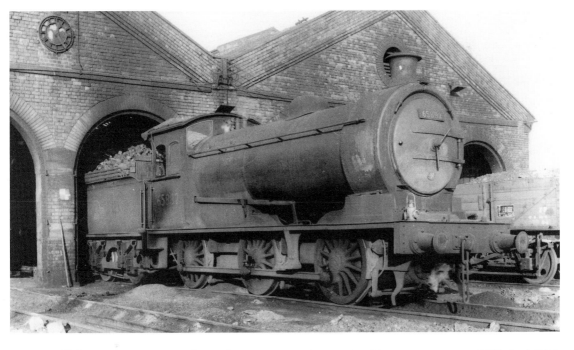

Just to the east of Middlesbrough on the way to Redcar and Saltburn is Haverton Hill shed 51G, virtually a goods loco shed only. J27 0–6–0 no. 65882 is typical of the engines shedded here.

Redcar, originally part of the Stockton & Darlington Railway, had its first station opened in 1846.
This early structure only lasted a short while. By 1861 the line through Redcar was under the
control of the LNER who built and opened a new station, Redcar Central. From Middlesbrough
to Redcar the line is never very far from the banks of the River Tees – not that there is much
chance of seeing the river as it is a very heavily industrialised area which includes a very large
British Steel complex.

BR standard class 4MT no. 76050 at the head of a race special, conveying passengers to Redcar's other
famous landmark: its racecourse.

On from Redcar is Saltburn, right on the coast. The line is a continuation of the original Stockton & Darlington line from Middlesbrough. With its station constructed under the guidance of Henry Pease, Saltburn was originally a Roman signal station, then a small fishing port. According to legend the town was full of smugglers but, with the coming of the railways, it developed into a Victorian seaside resort, complete with pier.

L1 2–6–4T no. 67777 near Saltburn with a stopping passenger train.

A5 4–6–2T no. 69832 shunting empty stock at Saltburn.

Back at Middlesbrough, our eastern expert tells us that a line leads off to Hartlepool, another eighteenth-century port that expanded when the railway reached the town. Before the main line arrived, there was a colliery line, built in 1823 to connect local pits. This line was built by Christopher Tennant of Yarm.

A3 no. 60086 *Gainsborough* travelling at good speed near Hartlepool carrying a 50B Leeds shedplate.

A3 4–6–2 no. 60100 *Spearmint* trundles a coal train through West Hartlepool.

Another coal train makes its way through West Hartlepool – this time it is J27 0–6–0 no. 65869. The trucks look a little antiquated, so perhaps it is a local working, as there are many mines in the area.

Another J27 photographed at the same location as the above is no. 65816. This time it looks as though it is hauling livestock vehicles.

While travelling on the train, I have certainly learned a lot more about the Eastern Region than I ever knew before thanks to the knowledge of our Eastern enthusiasts. By way of photographs in the archive, we have seen the areas east and west of the East Coast Main Line and the variety of locomotives that operate in those areas. Here are three views of Gresley A3s on the main line north of Darlington.

A3 4–6–2 no. 60056 *Centenary*.

This A3 with small smoke deflectors by the chimney is no. 60061 *Pretty Polly*, named after a race horse – not a parrot!

A3 no. 60105 *Victor Wild*.

After leaving Darlington there is fine countryside but not much for the railway enthusiasts to see, so it is once more out with the refreshments – or what is left of them – and we settle down and chat. As any railway enthusiast knows, a journey by train goes from frantic activity, trying not to miss anything, to periods of looking out of the windows and wondering what steam engines the next station will produce. And, of course, all the time there is constant talk about railways, which fellow enthusiasts will understand but lesser mortals will condemn us as anoraks with a very low IQ.

V2 2–6–2 no. 60971, a 1936 Gresley design, on the main line north of Darlington.

We shall shortly be going through Aycliffe non-stop. We probably won't see anything that we can take a photograph of, so we shall press our noses against the windows and take notes instead. After Aycliffe, we pass under the Stockton to Shildon and Bishop Auckland line, then comes Bradbury and Ferryhill. Looking at the map that has been produced by one of our group, Ferryhill seems to be a major junction of lines: Hartlepool to Bishop Auckland, Ferryhill to Sunderland and, of course, the East Coast Main Line to Durham. Ferryhill was an early medieval settlement and gradually evolved to become a mining area. With the coming of the railways in 1840, a large blast furnace was built, setting the stage for the growth of Ferryhill.

G5 0–4–4T no. 67263 near Sunderland on a local passenger train.

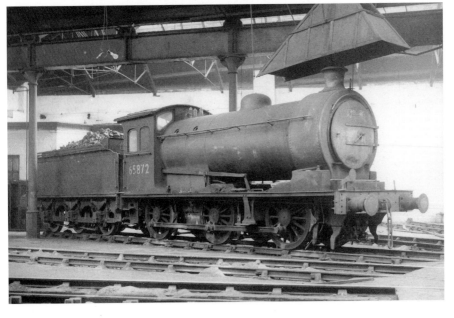

Sunderland 54A shed is home to J27 0–6–0 no. 65872.

J26 no. 65841 works a heavy mineral train near Sunderland. Shipbuilding was an important industry in Sunderland as early as the fourteenth century. It was also a major shipping port for coal and salt. Sunderland also holds an unfortunate distinction of being one of the most heavily bombed areas during the Second World War.

V1 2–6–2T no. 67639, carrying express headlamps, is photographed on a summer's day in the suburbs of Sunderland in 1953.

On the opposite bank of the River Wear to Sunderland is Monkwearmouth. Back in the 1840s there was no bridge between Sunderland and Monkwearmouth. George Hudson, the 'Railway King' as he was known, and before his fall from grace, was elected MP for Sunderland in 1845. Being such a dominant figure, he wanted to build a grand station at Monkwearmouth to go with his status as MP for Sunderland, and who would argue with him? So a grand station he had, with Doric columns and a portico in a style to match his flamboyant character. At the time it suited him, but no doubt there were many that thought it too a high a price for a small railway, although his strength of will has left Monkwearmouth with a lovely station.

G5 0–4–4T no. 67251 of 1894 with a local stopping train at Monkwearmouth.

North of Monkwearmouth is the River Tyne with its vast industrial complexes of Boldon, South Shields, Jarrow, Pelaw and Tyne Dock to name but a few. Tyne Dock 54B is home shed to some of the heaviest freight locos in the country. This view is of Q7 0–8–0 no. 63469, weighing in at 116 tons. With a tractive effort of 37,000lb, it could handle very heavy coal and ore trains.

Another elderly tank loco is J72 no. 68687 of 1898 vintage, seen here on the Tyne Dock shed with a couple of youngsters, in the shape of BR 9F 2–10–0s, for company.

Class T 4–8–0 no. 69914 shunting in the Tyne Dock area in 1953.

Q7 0–8–0 no. 63463 awaits duty on Tyne Dock shed in 1956. Its stable companion is O1 2–8–0 no. 63760.

V1 2–6–2T no. 67673 between Brockley Whins and Boldon with a Middlesbrough–Newcastle train in 1956.

Back on the main line again, we shall soon be into Durham. The station is built at the end of a viaduct. Our Eastern enthusiast friend tells us that from the carriage window, when on the viaduct, we shall have a superb view of Durham Castle and the cathedral. He also gives us some information about the viaduct. Built the same as the station and with ten arches, it crosses the Wear Gorge and dominates the east of the city of Durham.

A1 4–6–2 no. 60147 *North Eastern* with 'The Queen of Scots' Pullman express near Durham in 1951.

This photograph is of another named express near Durham. It is A3 4–6–2 no. 60085 *Manna* with 'The Heart of Midlothian'. Manna was a 1920s St Leger-winning racehorse.

Consett, with its huge steelworks, is one of the reasons why so many heavyweight locomotives are shedded in the area; they work the ore and coal trains. There is also a viaduct crossing the valley which is adjacent to the steelworks which was built in 1858 for the Stockton & Darlington Railway. The engineer and designer was Thomas Bouch, it is 250 yards long and has twelve arches with a maximum height of 150ft. After the Tay Bridge disaster, Thomas Bouch fell from favour and it was decided to build additional buttresses to support the viaduct, just in case!

Q6 0–8–0 no. 63342, coaled and watered, waits patiently on Consett shed 54D for its next call of duty.

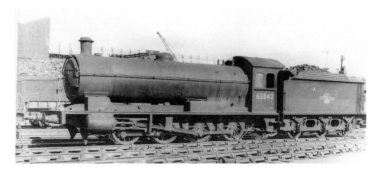

Another Q6, no. 63437, looks as though it could be waiting for a service in this 1957 view.

Q6 no. 63387 with a rather battered chimney. It looks in need of some tender loving care.

We are nearing the end of our Eastern journey now, but there are still a few locations to look at before we roll to a stop in Newcastle. As we near Newcastle, there is a junction to the left at Low Fell to a most important area; a few miles along this line is Blaydon, another heavy freight shed, and then Wylam.

K1 2–6–0 no. 62044 ready for duty on Blaydon shed 52C.

J94 0–6–0ST no. 68036, photographed on Blaydon shed. This class of loco was built during the Second World War to a Riddles design for the Ministry of Supply. After the war, in 1946, the LNER bought them.

Another K1, no. 62010, also on Blaydon shed looking rather grimy. It appears to be leaking around the chimney.

Richard Trevithick has quite rightly been accredited for inventing the moving steam engine, but Wylam is where the modern railway was born. One of Trevithick's early engines of 1805 was tried on the Wylam Waggonway, hauling several waggons of coal. The track, however, which was wood on stone blocks, could not support the weight of the locomotive and not much was heard of this experiment again.

I used the words 'the modern railway was born' deliberately as the 1780s saw the birth of two baby boys in Wylam who would transform travel worldwide – namely George Stephenson in 1781 and Timothy Hackworth in 1786. George Stephenson was born in a cottage by the side of the waggonway from Wylam Colliery. His father was a fireman at the colliery, so it was only natural he would follow in his father's footsteps and he joined Wylam Colliery at the age of thirteen. In 1805 he moved to Killingworth Colliery where eventually he was put in charge of all the machinery. It was during his time at Killingworth that George built his first loco, *Blucher*. It was fitted with flanged wheels so that it could run on rails as we know them today. It was about this time that Edward Pease, the prime mover of the Stockton & Darlington Railway, heard of George Stephenson and they met in 1821. At this meeting, Stephenson was asked if he would do a survey for the Stockton & Darlington line using the most direct route possible, which was not easy in those days due to most of the land belonging to the so-called gentry who either did not want the line on their land or they were money-grabbing and held out for as much as they could get. The line was eventually opened and the inaugural run took place on 27 September 1825. The line also set the track gauge of 4ft 8in, being the same as the Wylam Waggonway. The extra half-inch was added later. *Locomotion No. 1* (as it has become known) headed the train of thirty-three trucks and coaches and averaged 8mph. It was a huge success watched by thousands all along the route. As the S&DR progressed, better and more powerful locomotives were needed and this is when Timothy Hackworth came to the fore. He had worked in collieries in the area and joined the Stephenson's Forth Street works in Newcastle. He had overseen the construction of *Locomotion* at the works and, when asked to design more powerful engines, he designed and built the *Royal George*. It was very successful and saved the reputation of the S&DR whose early engines suffered many breakdowns. By 1832 there were nineteen locos at work on the Stockton & Darlington. Another engineer, although not born in Wylam but who was educated there, was William Hedley. He designed and built *Puffing Billy*, a name known by millions of schoolchildren in years gone by.

North Wylam station opened in 1876. The earlier station of Wylam was opened in 1835 on the Newcastle–Carlisle line.

Further on from Wylam on the Newcastle–Carlisle line, which dates from 1835, is Hexham. An abbey was founded in AD 674 and through the years the town grew as a social centre. It's very much an agricultural area and, with the coming of the railways, it became a very popular country resort for the Newcastle gentry. Photographed leaving Hexham is G5 0–4–4T no. 67309.

On from Hexham, through Fourstones, Haydon Bridge and Bardon Mill, comes Haltwhistle. This is now a very rural area, and at Haltwhistle is a branch line heading south to the terminus at Alston. Haltwhistle is very popular with hill walkers, as Hadrian's Wall is just to the north of the railway line. This view is of G5 0–4–4T no. 67315 at the terminus at Alston.

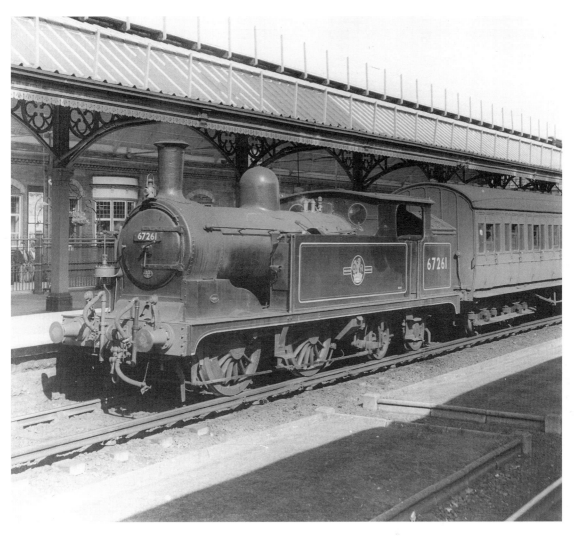

We are getting very close now to the end of our Eastern journey, and we just have time to mention a few locations. Just outside Newcastle is Monkseaton at the mouth of the Tyne near Whitley Bay. G5 0–4–4T no. 67261 rests at a Monkseaton platform with a local stopping train.

Another station not far from the East Coast is Newsham, a bit further north than the end of our journey at Newcastle. Our expert friend tells us that it was an interesting station as it was the junction for North and South Blyth. Here, G5 0–4–4T no. 67261 is seen dropping off passengers at Newsham.

South Blyth shed in the 1920s.

J27 0–6–0 no. 65804 is being coaled at North Blyth shed.

J21 0–6–0 no. 65033, a veteran of 1886 and designed by T.W. Worsdell for the NER, was still at work in 1959 and is resting here on South Blyth shed.

The principal shed for supplying locos to Newcastle is Gateshead 52A. Once a major works built by the NER, locomotives were built here until 1908 and, in the words of our expert, the works were moved lock, stock and barrel to Darlington. The railway was very important to the coal mines in the area, and coal staithes were built on the south bank of the Tyne. The railway was vital in conveying coal from the mines to these staithes for export.

Q7 0–8–0 no. 63471 working a train of empties through Gateshead.

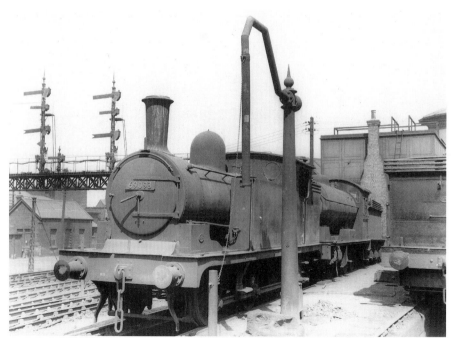

N10 0–6–2T no. 69093 at rest on Gateshead shed.

Another view at Gateshead is of G5 0–4–4T no. 67343.

Inside Gateshead shed; this time it's J72 no. 69005 photographed in 1958, built in 1897. In this picture it looks as good as new after sixty years of service.

On the opposite side of the River Tyne from Gateshead is another important shed to Newcastle – Heaton – with its many freight engines and passenger locos. The freight is mainly for working the docks and the coalfields, which are prolific in the Newcastle area.

V1 2–6–2T no. 67635 with an inspection carriage at Heaton in 1952.

Heavyweight freight engine B16 4–6–0 no. 61447, heads what looks like a rake of empty coal waggons through Heaton.

Forming the background to a driver and fireman looking for their engine are two V1s, nos 67652 and 67683, on Heaton shed.

It's hard work pushing the 160-ton A1 4–6–2 *Aboyeur* around on the Heaton turntable. In this 1952 view of no. 60148, it has the early unlipped chimney.

Another A1 on the Heaton shed – this time no. 60136 *Alcazar* with a lipped chimney, which was much more appropriate for these quality engines.

Our train is slowing now; there is a squeal of flanges on rails and very little sound from our A3, with just the occasional beat of the exhaust to be heard as the driver carefully controls his speed to approach Robert Stephenson's high level bridge, opened in 1849. It is a two-level bridge with a roadway beneath the railway. We are now on the bridge and a slight increase in the exhaust beat keeps up steady speed to get us to the end of our journey. We are all at the windows, looking down at the Tyne 120ft below us, marvelling that a bridge of over 100 years can still stand up to the weight of the modern trains. Our locomotive alone was probably heavier than most trains in those early days. Off the bridge, and we are slowing for the station; now all eyes are on what locomotives we may see.

Station pilot at Newcastle is J72 no. 68680, looking very smart in this late 1950s view.

C12 4–4–2T no. 67394 standing in Newcastle station with a local train.

With a squeal of brakes, we come to a halt and, with the familiar clanging and banging of doors, we are on the platform. Newcastle started as a fort on Hadrian's Wall. It was in the nineteenth century that the city grew. The advent of the Stephensons and the railways really saw good times. Robert Stephenson built the high level bridge in 1849 and Lord Armstrong built the swing bridge in 1876. Shipbuilding became the key industry in the city. Central station was built in 1850 for the York, Newcastle and Berwick Railway. The architects were Robert Stephenson and John Dobson. Dobson has been credited with designing much of the centre of Newcastle. Newcastle Central was the first station built with a great arched roof. There are three arched spans of some 60ft-wide, the central one reaching higher than the other two. The station is built on a curve but during the ensuing years there have been changes. As the city prospered so did the railway and more platforms had to be added. The opening of the station in 1850 was a royal event with Queen Victoria and Prince Albert performing the official ceremony. This event is commemorated at the station – if you lift your eyes above the entrance to the refreshment room you will see the carved faces of the royal couple!

A1 4–6–2 no. 60119 *Patrick Stirling* at rest in Newcastle Central.

With clear signals, A3 no. 60085 *Manna* eases out of the platform at Newcastle.

A visitor from Scotland, D30 4–4–0 no. 62428 *The Talisman* at Newcastle Central.

Heading south from Newcastle is A2 no. 60526 *Sugar Palm* showing clearly the magnificent roof of the station. Waiting for clear signals on an adjacent line at the head of a freight train is J39 no. 64704.

Our Eastern journey is now over. We may have soot on our faces and hands and are feeling a little tired, but we all feel a reluctance to leave the atmosphere of the station. With the sounds of doors slamming, the station announcer telling travellers where the next train is going to and a gleaming A4 standing at the platform, like a racehorse waiting for the off, what railway enthusiast would want to leave? But leave we must. As with our other journeys, I hope you have enjoyed accompanying us and have learnt a little about the places we have visited.

A4 no. 60005 *Sir Charles Newton*, named after the chief general manager of the LNER, about to leave Newcastle Central.